Style
Diaries

SIMONE WERLE

Style
Diaries

World Fashion from Berlin to Tokyo

PRESTEL
MUNICH · BERLIN · LONDON · NEW YORK

Content

Not so long ago, the fashion thing was cut and dried. Trends were created four times a year on the world's most important catwalks and then delivered to the public in glossy fashion magazines. Only very rarely, when a spirit of rebellion was in the air, would fashion be momentarily dragged down from its lofty throne. But whether it was the hippie style, mod, or punk, thanks to the catwalk any subversive trend would be quickly ironed out and made palatable to the masses. Whatever was happening in the world's closets, it was all the same to fashion, for fashion claimed the right to dictate what garments should be hanging there. For the last few years, however, the fashion network no longer extends only to Paris, Milan, and New York. Fashion is everywhere. How did this happen? Quite simply — a few boys, girls, men, and women began to show the world who they are.

The ingredients to this revolution in clothing are rather simple. A blog, a camera, and a healthy dose of personal style have proven to be more than enough for the democratization of fashion. Eccentric looks and genuine wit have helped both female and male fashion bloggers earn millions of fans worldwide, and to easily stay at least a season ahead of the trendsetting fashion industry. At a time when the collective attention span is shrinking and there is a greater yearning for real signs of authenticity, fashion blogs might not (yet) be the biggest stars on the fashion firmament, but they are certainly the brightest. What these private fashion diaries lack (or so the industry says) in broad expertise and marketing muscle they more than make up for in creativity, determination, and the guts to be different. Fashion blogs are not only the most visible arm of the indie fashion scene, they are a cultural phenomenon that show just how quickly established structures can be broken down. Rarely has it been so much fun watching a revolution happen.

Simone Werle

SHANNON LICARI

BORN 1983 | AMERICAN | CITY: MINNEAPOLIS | WWW.SEEKINGDIRTYHAIRHALO.BLOGSPOT.COM

SHANNON LICARI

I'm a Northern California transplant living in Minneapolis, Minnesota. People think that's crazy. I already know. ◆ I stretch the boundaries of my office dress code with a mix of thrifted and new clothing, add a dash of bohemia and a pinch of rock. My job? Boring in this employer's market of an economy, so each day has become another day to get dressed (not boring). ◆ My signature style is bohemian rock chick with a little sugar. ◆ I'm an experimental eater. So far the only thing I hate are gibsons. They truly make me gag, but I keep trying. ◆ I'm currently on the hunt for massive bell bottoms. MASSIVE. ◆ Music is my religion and I love attending shows and music festivals. ◆ I still watch America's Funniest Home Videos. Hilarious. ◆ I'm a mix of Filipino, French, and Native American. I've enjoyed being ethnically indiscernible. ◆ Show me fringe, feathers, floral prints, or brocade and I commence drooling. ◆ One of my favorite things to do is put items together that have no business with each other and see what kind of weird baby they can have. ◆ I take my own pictures using a tripod and remote shutter release. I hide this narcissism in back alleys and behind buildings, all the while flaunting it on my blog. ◆ I'm a Gemini. I'm also a twin. What's up now, Cosmos? ◆ I avoid full-on belly-bearing shirts. I cover that shit up for a reason. ◆ Silhouette and proportion are top priorities. ◆ More jewelry is more better. ◆ I have two cats: Marzipan and Kola, they're my babies.

Bared a little midriff under this sheer peplum flap of a shirt thing. Something about stretching the boundaries of my office dress code is so tempting.

KRYSTAL SIMPSON

BORN 1982 | AMERICAN | CITY: SALINAS, CALIFORNIA / NEW YORK | WWW.WHATISREALITYANYWAY.COM

KRYSTAL SIMPSON

{ 14 THINGS ABOUT MYSELF }

I don't like condiments or salad dressing. ◆ Freddie Mercury was my first crush. ◆ I'm secretly good at skateboarding, baseball, basketball, hockey, and riding motorcycles. ◆ I once picked out Steven Tyler's (of Aerosmith) stage outfit before a concert. ◆ I was on an MTV reality show. ◆ I would never wear uncomfortable heels. ◆ I can ride a unicycle. ◆ I'm the singer of the Little Feather band. ◆ The key piece of my wardrobe are my men's YSL boots. ◆ I'm an award-winning poet and writer. ◆ I've always been a tomboy, and I don't like to be uncomfortable. I am really attracted to women that look a bit androgynous, I find it so sexy. ◆ My blog is my public diary. ◆ My mother called me only by my middle name Annie, but called me Krystal when I was in trouble, and my friends call me Krys or Kryssie. ◆ I love quantum physics.

Living the most
exciting life
possible is my
goal, and it's easy
to have, if you just
follow whatever
it is you love to do
— my motto
is if it's not fun
don't do it.

EDWARD HONAKER

BORN 1993 | AMERICAN | CITY: SAN DIEGO | HTTP://LOOKBOOK.NU/USER/69091-EDWARD-H

EDWARD HONAKER

{ 11 THINGS ABOUT MYSELF }

I'm in my last year of high school, so studying takes up a lot of my time, although not nearly as much as it should. ◆ I work part time at a Tae Kwon Do studio, where I teach TKD to kids and adults. It's honestly the weirdest job ever. ◆ I have two sisters, a brother, and two wonderful parents. I was fortunate enough to have a dad that taught me how to shine my shoes and a brother that taught me how to tie a tie and a sister to tell me when I looked like an idiot. I also have tons of extended family, and they all live close, so the weekends are interesting, to say the least. ◆ At my church, I'm in charge of recording the sermons, archiving them, and uploading them to the Internet. ◆ I probably spend more time fixing my hair than the average teenage girl does, and my idea of a wild Saturday night is polishing my brown shoes with black polish. ◆ I like wearing suits a lot, and I almost exclusively wear leather shoes these days. I've always wanted to put on my best suit, shirt, tie, and shoes, and go to someplace like Denny's, just for kicks. ◆ I talk way too much for my own good, but I also really like making people smile and laugh. I try to make at least one person laugh each day. It's one of my rules. ◆ Sometimes I like to take my dog, Molly, for walks, but most of the time she avoids me. Maybe it's my cologne. ◆ I really like the styles of the 1940s through the 1960s. Everyone always looked so clean, with tucked-in shirts, neatly combed hair, and polished leather shoes. It seems that people back then always made an effort to look respectful and presentable, even when just running errands, and I think that's pretty admirable. ◆ I disagree with the notion that "there are no rules in fashion," but I also don't like when people follow rules to the letter. It's all about balance. Usually, rules have a good reason behind them, and once you understand that reason, then you can go about breaking the rule, respectful, of course. ◆ I once had a dream that I was going to meet up with a friend, and I was getting dressed, but I couldn't decide on which color socks to wear. I was really stressed out about it, so I woke up all nervous and restless. That can't be healthy.

I'm not much of a fan of sneakers in general. I think they are worn too much, and rather inappropriately. Of course, they have their time and place, but it's important to remember that time and place is not, contrary to popular belief, all the time.

AYA SMITH

AMERICAN | CITY: BLOOMINGTON, INDIANA | WWW.STRAWBERRYKOI.BLOGSPOT.COM

AYA SMITH

{ 6 THINGS ABOUT MYSELF }

I've been officially wearing vintage items for two years, but I always had a fondness for antiques and vintage things while growing up. ◆ I was married at 19 years old ... I'm 24 now and we just celebrated our 5-year anniversary. ◆ Between the two of us, we have one child — a beautiful son, named Lucien Akira Alexander. ◆ I am a Japanese/German mix of heritage. I have been to both Germany and Japan and I do speak Japanese although I do not speak German. ◆ My pictures are taken by Thomas Smith, my husband and personal photographer. ◆ I'm a Sagittarius.

Strawberry Koi,
a fruit, a fish, a
color, an emotion,
Love. The name is
an analogy of the
person that I am.

SUSANNA LAU

BORN 1983 | BRITISH | CITY: LONDON | WWW.STYLEBUBBLE.TYPEPAD.COM

SUSANNA LAU

{ 11 THINGS ABOUT MYSELF }

I'm British-born Chinese by way of Hong Kong — though often get mistaken for being Japanese/Korean by fellow Hong Kongers. ✦ I grew up eating my way around the world because my parents are obsessed foodies — I will literally try everything and anything. Kangaroo steaks? Yum. Fried cicadas? Hmmm, hmmm. ✦ I have a disturbing weakness for period dramas — especially BBC ones! ✦ I had two hamsters named Bobble and Bubble, after the arcade game — they ended up killing each other though, and when they died I buried one under the apple tree and the other under the pear tree — I thought they'd be happier by themselves. ✦ I went all the way through primary school thinking I was a high achiever but then got to secondary school and realized that I was actually quite a mediocrity. ✦ My love of fashion was initially an act of rebellion against my parents and the "popular" people at school — which then developed into something all-consuming and now is my number one passion. ✦ I take up tons of craft, DIY projects, and other creative things only to leave them half finished and botched up — this is something I'm working on! ✦ I have 3 younger sisters — we are all wildly different, but are all outcasts in our own little ways. ✦ My parents met in an airport and fell in love at first sight — they have a sickeningly together/stable marriage. Thus, the bar has been raised too high and I in turn have NO faith in love whatsoever. ✦ Susie Bubble wasn't made up by myself, it was my friend Sarah Hill at primary school that gave it to me. Then the whole class started calling me that — it's because I always looked like I was in a world of my own, in a BUBBLE! I have not really grown out of this — you will often see me staring into space, fixated at nothing in particular, or listening to my iPod oblivious to many things. ✦ My interests are macaroons from Laduree, art shows with killer paintings or artists with killer instincts, and all things killer. Oh, and I like looking at the sea, because the sea likes looking back at me!! Penguin classics anniversary books, shoes with a good sturdy heel, and shimmery makeup. I like eating anything with red beans, garlic butter, and nuts (not necessarily all at once). I like seeing films that have killer lines, killer gigs, Amelia's magazine, feathers and lace ...

I'd say that I'm creative in odd ways ...
unfortunately not skilled though.

KAYLA HADLINGTON

BORN 1993 | BRITISH | CITY: BIRMINGHAM | WWW.KAYLAHADLINGTON.BLOGSPOT.COM

KAYLA HADLINGTON

{ 17 THINGS ABOUT MYSELF }

I like to shop in charity shops. ◆ I like to make my own clothes. ◆ I want to be a designer when I'm older OR I want to open my own shop and sell handmade, one-off clothes OR I want to sell vintage clothes and have a vintage shop. ◆ I want to do a mixture of all three! ◆ I like to reconstruct old clothes. ◆ I've got an obsession with vintage clothes. ◆ I didn't take textiles or fashion at GCSE because I didn't have the option, so instead I took fine art and graphics which I have an A* and A in. ◆ My mom taught me how to sew. ◆ I'm learning how to draft patterns. ◆ I'm only 5' 3". ◆ Usually I have an idea everyday of what I'm going to wear when I wake up, sometimes I make it up in my mind before I go to sleep, however when it comes to getting dressed I put on the clothes I was thinking of, then change my mind and begin to start madly getting everything out of my wardrobe, flinging it on, then looking in the mirror, pulling it off again, and putting something else on until I find something I'm happy with — which is probably how I find my best and worst outfits. ◆ I can draw and paint. ◆ I love Harry Potter. ◆ I spend most my time on Lookbook posting my outfits, my blog, or Tumblr. ◆ My blog is somewhere I can share what I think about clothes with other people, post pictures of my outfits, things I have purchased, tutorials, and show people that you can find amazing things in charity shops. ◆ I am the admin of a Harry Potter Forum and have been for 5 years now. ◆ I'm very good with graphic design.

When I'm feeling lazy, or I haven't got much time, I find it easy to put on a pair of leggings, an oversized vintage man's shirt, and a belt.

JAMES ANDREW

BORN 1962 | AMERICAN | CITY: NEW YORK | WWW.WHATISJAMESWEARING.COM

JAMES ANDREW

I'm an interior designer, and a fashion and lifestyle advisor. ✦ I continually strive to be a better version of myself. ✦ I've never settled for little fantasies. ✦ One of the most rewarding things for me is helping people realize their dreams. ✦ I've recently been described as a cross between Diana Vreeland, Auntie Mame, and Deepak Chopra. ✦ I want to make a movie. ✦ With my blog I really try to create a total sensory experience for my readership based on my passion for elevated living. ✦ My clothes are an expression of who I am. ✦ I love to dress up rather than down. ✦ The best purchase I ever made is a painting that now hangs over my sofa — it's an incredibly handsome work that once belonged to the legendary designer Billy Baldwin ... and I found it at a junk shop! ✦ As a designer, I'm proud to be making the world a prettier place one room at a time. ✦ One should never say "never," but I haven't had the occasion or desire yet to wear any sort of animal print. ✦ I approach my day as if I were directing a movie — creating a total picture — which of course includes coordinating what I'm wearing with where I'll be going, who I'll be seeing, and the kind of vibe I want to create. ✦ As a rule I try to come from a place of joy and fearlessness. ✦ I've never had a problem with celebrating who I am.

I believe we create
our own reality.

ULRIKE SCHUMANN

BORN 1981 | GERMAN | CITY: ZÜRICH | WWW.DOTTISDOTS.BLOGSPOT.COM

ULRIKE SCHUMANN

{ 16 THINGS ABOUT MYSELF }

My real name is Ulrike, but nobody calls me that way. Dotti is a nickname I once was given due to all the polka dot dresses I used to wear. Nowadays most of these dresses were exchanged for gingham pieces, but the name stayed. ◆ Originally I'm from Berlin. A few years ago I was fed up with the city and moved on to Hamburg. A bit later I met my boy and left Hamburg for Munich, which is 1,000 km south. It's a nice place, but then we moved on to Switzerland, which turned out to be even nicer. That's why we're here now. ◆ I'm a person that takes nearly all important decisions by gut. ◆ I was born in the former German Democratic Republic. And even though I had a nice childhood I am so happy that these times are over. ◆ I have a room full of dresses and the nicest vintage things, but only wear a few pieces regularly. ◆ I like going to bed early and getting up early. It makes me happier then sleeping all day long. ◆ My favorite colors are pink, red, and navy. ◆ I love ironing. ◆ I used to be a writer for German music television and a copywriter in advertising. But I decided to quit this job in order to do what I am more passionate about: vintage clothing. ◆ I always win when I play backgammon. ◆ I want to have a wire-haired dachshund. ◆ I get inspired by kitschy old alpine movies, fashion photography from the 50s and 60s, series like Mad Men. But I always try to add a modern twist with basics and pieces from my favorite labels, since I don't want to look like a 100% replication from former times. ◆ I could go crazy for lovely color combinations. ◆ The key pieces of my wardrobe are 50s dresses, sailor-style dresses, dirndl dresses, and gingham dresses. ◆ I would like to have a milk cow and goats and chickens and an herb garden. ◆ I like meat. Also the pieces of meat many people don't like — e.g., cow tongue and calf liver — because I think you should utilize a living being completely when you've killed it and not throw away the other half. And I always watch out to buy organic and regional and eat meat only once or twice a week.

Just one more blog about this and that and fashion and eating and ponies and the weather and nonsense.

YOKOO

AMERICAN | CITY: ATLANTA | WWW.FLICKR.COM/PHOTOS/YOKOOYOKOO

YOKOO

{ 8 THINGS ABOUT MYSELF }

I am still afraid of the dark. ◆ I could eat Chinese food every day of the week. ◆ I do not own a pair of heels. ◆ I have seen every single episode of Alfred Hitchcock Presents. ◆ I do not draw. ◆ Two of my favorite things: vintage magazines with amazing covers and Swatch watches. ◆ I am not what you would call a "girly girl." ◆ I only recently learned how to apply eyeliner, from a tutorial on YouTube.

Losing your creativity is like losing your Mojo!
Use it or lose it!

ESZTER FARKAS

BORN 1977 | AUSTRIAN | CITY: VIENNA | WWW.STYLORECTIC.BLOGSPOT.COM

ESZTER FARKAS

{ 15 THINGS ABOUT MYSELF }

I was born in Budapest. ◆ I am introverted/extroverted. ◆ I am very chaotic but I also need an accurate plan for each day. ◆ To be honest I don't like being photographed. ◆ I changed my residence 10 times so far. ◆ I still have no driver's license. ◆ As a child I counted everything I saw. ◆ The longest I've gone without sleeping was 4 days. ◆ My pictures are taken by my beloved and patient boyfriend ... yeah, I can get pretty grumpy in some situations. ◆ It might be that I burst into tears when I see old people eat. ◆ I worry way too much, even though I know I shouldn't. ◆ I love cats. Forever. Always. ◆ I am not the most elegant person around. I like a bit more tougher clothes. ◆ My blog really grew on me. It's a hobby, a distraction, and an outlet for eszterish things. It keeps me entertained and also kinda busy and I am thankful for that as I always need something to do or I go nuts. ◆ I am not into real fur.

I cried, I cheered, I feared, I laughed, and yeah, all of this simultaneously.

ADRIÁN CANO

BORN 1989 | SPANISH | CITY: BRIGHTON | WWW.ITSADRIANCANO.BLOGSPOT.COM

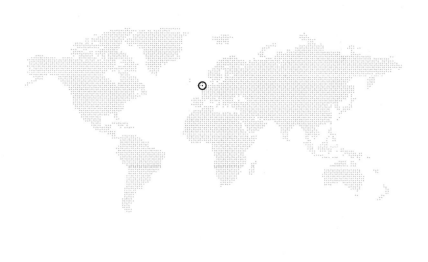

ADRIÁN CANO

I am from Granada (Spain) but I moved to Brighton (United Kingdom) to study English at the University of Sussex. ◆ I am a random guy who loves everything that is related with art. Cinema and photography are my passions. I can just spend lots of days watching films, especially independent cinema. ◆ Literature is quite important in my life. I think that a good story or a poem well written could share a moment more than anything else. I do love to write; I use it as a tool to show my subconscious mind and to be able to preserve that feeling for each time I want to read it. ◆ The best moments in your life are always the cheapest ones. Apart from being with good friends, you can also enjoy your life looking at the poetry that is in the world. You just need to know where to find it. ◆ I love homemade paella, especially the one my mother cooks for me every time I'm back home. About drinks, it might seem weird but I do love cold milk with sugar, orange and tropical juice. And I couldn't live without chocolate! ◆ I love the smart look with a vintage touch. I love people who dress very sharp. ◆ I do not have any differentiation between clothes for going out and clothes for everyday life. You can find me wearing a sharp mod-style suit with shirt, tie, and a hat on the streets at noon; and going out with a basic t-shirt and skinny jeans. ◆ I am not the kind of guy who is into blogs of trendy people or style icons. I catch up on ideas from the people I come across on the streets.

I want to show not only my life, but also my point of view about everything that is happening. Hope you like it.

HOMAKO

BORN 1982 | JAPANESE | CITY: LOS ANGELES | WWW.FLICKR.COM/HOMAKO

HOMAKO

I was born in Japan and studied fashion design in Tokyo. ◆ I can't say NO to polka dots and stripes. ◆ With my blog, I want to make people smile, be happy, and even laugh. ◆ I worked for a designer in Antwerp, Belgium. ◆ I travel/jump/smile around many countries. Especially Europe. ◆ I love to give my own name to everything — people, plants, foods, cameras, clothes. ◆ I am a candy- and ice cream-holic. ◆ I collect Gummies and I found out they stay good for up to 3 years. ◆ Now I live in Los Angeles with my husband who I married on an island. ◆ I have a hair monster daughter dog named Poppin. ◆ I try not to think about what other people think. ◆ When I am on a date with my husband Ryan, I try to match with his clothes' color. ◆ I love taking photos and doing many art projects with my sister Sayaka and my friends. ◆ I usually shop at vintage stores, Etsy shops, and flea markets. ◆ My real name is Yoko Minemura Vega, but I am known as HOMAKO.

AUDREY LEIGHTON ROGERS

BORN 1988 | AMERICAN | CITY: LONDON | WWW.BEFRASSY.COM

AUDREY LEIGHTON ROGERS

{ 16 THINGS ABOUT MYSELF }

I'm American. ◆ I speak Spanish. ◆ I have obsessions with poetry and photography. ◆ I drink far too much caffeine and am almost always wearing some sort of blazer. ◆ I'm very loud, probably too loud. ◆ Long summer nights and sun-kissed skin are two of life's best pleasures. ◆ I have an incredibly addictive personality. ◆ Edie Sedgwick has been my fashion icon since I was about 12. ◆ I adore language and I love photography; when I was initially introduced to the blogosphere, I was inspired to combine these two hobbies and then channel them into what I thrive on: fashion. ◆ Blazers with gold buttons and sharp tailoring and a couple vintage furs from Paris are the key pieces of my wardrobe. ◆ I don't like delicate heels, but prefer big chunky platforms that hide my abnormally skinny ankles. ◆ I write for anyone, everyone who values clothes and the creativity that lies behind the simple act of "getting dressed." ◆ If I spend too long deciding what to wear, I enter a self-inflicted panic-frenzy, where I pull everything out of my wardrobe in desperation. To avoid that, I give myself a timed 20 minutes where I swiftly put together what I want to wear. Too much time and an ensemble will be ruined — most likely over-accessorized or overly layered. Spontaneity is the key to good dressing. ◆ Most of what I wear is vintage or customized. ◆ Positive commentary from my followers makes me smile, every time. ◆ Finally, I eat a lot of fruit.

A friend of mine took one look at me in this and said, "You couldn't look more like ... yourself."

LJUPKA KOHORTA

BORN 1988 | CROATIAN | CITY: OSIJEK/ZAGREB | WWW.GUERRILLAGIRL.NET

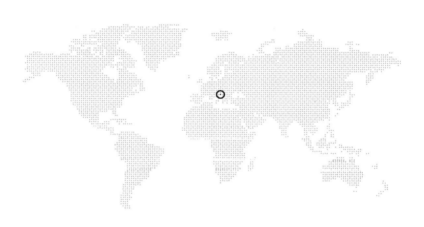

LJUPKA KOHORTA

{ 16 THINGS ABOUT MYSELF }

The thing that moves me the most is music. ◆ My favorite bands are Joy Division, Interpol, and The National. ◆ I am a student of defectology, but I spend most of my free time on any kind of fashion. ◆ I like movies and going to the movies alone to a small, local cinema, back row. ◆ My favorite movies are Clockwork Orange, Amelie, and Stray Dogs. ◆ I find Russia very interesting, so I collect Matryoshka dolls. ◆ I'd like to show the world that we can all be models, no matter the "size." ◆ I have no brothers or sisters. ◆ I don't like seeing bare skin at −15°C — health first! ◆ I live in Osijek, a small town (but big in Croatian terms). ◆ I have a dog named Mars; he's a golden retriever. ◆ I like autumn and the color gray. ◆ I don't like the seaside and am afraid of the fishes. ◆ I don't like cars, but adore bicycles and trains. ◆ I like poppies by the train rails, and I find the train station to be the happiest and saddest place in the world. ◆ I am a Chocoholic.

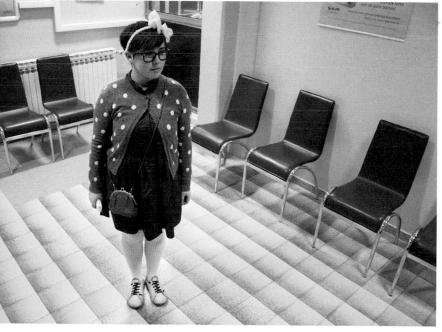

I'm a sad pony guerilla girl.

ELLE-MAY LECKENBY

BORN 1993 | AUSTRALIAN | SUNSHINE COAST, AUSTRALIA | HTTP://ELLE-MAYL.BLOGSPOT.COM

ELLE-MAY LECKENBY

{ 13 THINGS ABOUT MYSELF }

I was born in Townsville, Queensland. ✦ I love the hot weather/summer. ✦ I am a born-again Christian. ✦ I create video clips in my head when I listen to music. ✦ I sing at the top of my lungs when I'm home alone. ✦ I love modern clothes with a 40s or 50s touch. ✦ I've always loved feminine things. Anything that will make me feel pretty and happy. ✦ I collect different kinds of erasers. ✦ I always talk to myself. ✦ I love pesto, camembert, and sun-dried tomato on toasted Turkish bread. ✦ When I dress I always start with hair and makeup so that when I'm deciding on what to wear I'll look better in it when I try it on. ✦ I would love to be an actual princess of a country. ✦ I LOVE FASHION PHOTOGRAPHY (bet you didn't know that).

My biggest smiles
are made up of
memories.
That's why it's
so important to
capture them.

CLÉMENT LOUIS MOMPACH

BORN 1990 | FRENCH | CITY: PARIS | WWW.CLEMENTLOUIS.CANALBLOG.COM

CLÉMENT LOUIS MOMPACH

{ 11 THINGS ABOUT MYSELF }

I'm a photographer since two years ago. My "Art" is based on recurring subjects such as: the aesthetization of Death, loneliness, fashion, and fragility. ◆ I recently moved to Paris to be a student in Duperré, which is a school based on stylism and art. ◆ I started to enjoy fashion thanks to photography. ◆ I take my inspirations from "gothic," "romanticism," and "dandyism" styles. I love dark clothing with handmade accents. ◆ I'm a fan of Vanessa Paradis. She's just the perfect one. But I love Edie Sedgwick and Charlotte Gainsbourg as well. ◆ I hate ballet shoes! ◆ I love Rick Owens and his way of having nomad "roots" mixed with dark and gothic style. He created a lot of fantastic pieces — to me he is fashion's God! ◆ I don't like the waves of fashion that everybody adopts. ◆ You are best dressed when you are being classy. ◆ In the evening I get dressed according to my day humor. I like tuning my humor and my clothes. ◆ I am: Creative, Perfectionist, Lunar, Morbid, Analyst, Worried, Shy, Whimsical, Conqueror, Funny.

I'm interested in the aesthetization of Death, loneliness, fashion, and fragility.

NICOLE WARNE

BORN 1989 | SOUTH KOREAN/JAPANESE | CITY: TERRIGAL | WWW.GARYPEPPERVINTAGE.BLOGSPOT.COM

NICOLE WARNE

{ 18 THINGS ABOUT MYSELF }

I run an online vintage store which specializes in selling exquisite vintage clothing called Gary Pepper Vintage Pty Ltd, which I also balance with my vintage accessory store, Gary Pepper Pieces, as well as running and maintaining my fashion blog. ◆ I'm half-Korean half-Japanese. ◆ I'm extremely sentimental and I believe in love. ◆ I drink too much tea. ◆ Even though my style is constantly changing I do know that I will be wearing vintage for decades to come. For me, vintage is not a trend — it's a way of living. ◆ I can't get up in the mornings. ◆ I want to live in New York and also Japan. ◆ I'd never wear real fur! ◆ I want to see the aurora borealis in my lifetime. ◆ I work 70-hour weeks. ◆ I'm constantly daydreaming. ◆ My blog provides an insight into not only who I am but also how I run my online business, so it is a very large part of my life. It reflects who I am as a person, so it is extremely important to me. ◆ I bought my first vintage item when I was 15. ◆ I always throw something together at the last minute, which keeps my outfits very interesting! ◆ One day I hope to own my own clothing line and chain of vintage boutiques. ◆ I have an eclectic sense of style that mixes vintage with high-end designers, and I am never without my signature red lips. ◆ My main inspiration comes from a mix of street-style websites. I admire people who have absolutely no fear with what they wear and play by their own rules. ◆ I dress for no one but myself.

The Gary Pepper girl is a Japanese pop star. Famous in her own right, admired by all. She is fun, quirky, confident, passionate, exuberant, and beautiful with an eclectic sense of style. A chameleon at heart, she changes her spots as many times as she can and makes friends wherever she goes. Life motto? The glass is half full. The Gary Pepper girl is really one of a kind.

JANE ALDRIDGE

BORN 1991 | AMERICAN | CITY: TROPHY CLUB, TEXAS | WWW.SEAOFSHOES.TYPEPAD.COM

JANE ALDRIDGE

{ 13 THINGS ABOUT MYSELF }

I live kind of in the middle of nowhere. ◆ I am very obsessed with collecting shoes and clothes. ◆ I prefer vintage clothes to new clothes. ◆ I love to travel. ◆ I love Texas the best though — people here aren't afraid to be weird. ◆ Besides clothes and shoes I collect Italo Disco music, plastic toys, blue underwear, vintage Paris Vogues, and marine biology books. ◆ I called my blog "Sea of Shoes" partly because I am obsessed with marine animals. ◆ I think everyone should have a blog. ◆ I'm shy. ◆ I spend way too much time online. ◆ I started blogging when I was fifteen because I was bored. None of my friends were into fashion. I have always felt passionate about collecting couture, and my friends were always a little contemptuous of this. I felt very isolated; it was my way of reaching out to people with similar interests. ◆ I've always felt it is important to research your favorite designers and I've collected a lot of inspiration this way. ◆ You should always have fabulous shoes.

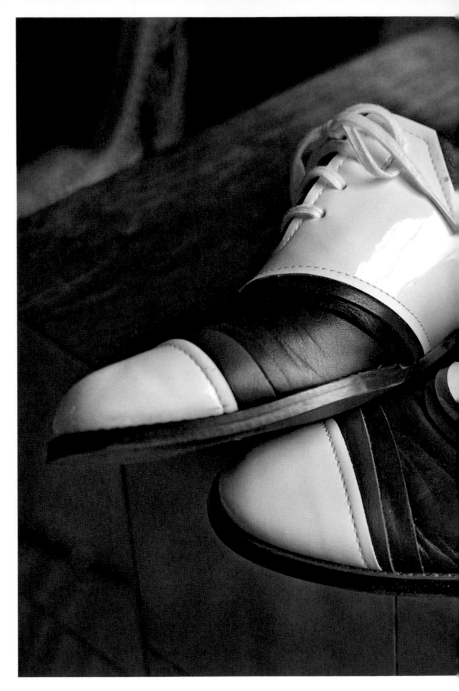

JENNIFER

BORN 1976 | AMERICAN | CITY: LANCASTER, PENNSYLVANIA | WWW.SALLYJANEVINTAGE.BLOGSPOT.COM

JENNIFER

{ 5 THINGS ABOUT MYSELF }

Ten things I like: Spanish moss hanging from live oaks, lens flare in my photos, a cat in my lap, singing at the top of my lungs in the car, the cold side of the pillow, Pillsbury orange rolls on Sunday morning, the smell of southern magnolias, polishing old shoes, eating with chopsticks, finding vintage photos with the names written on the back. ◆ My favorite decades are the 30s and 60s, especially the silhouettes and details of those eras. ◆ I think the only fashion rule I tend to stick to is if you wore it the first time, you shouldn't wear it the second time around. I spent the early 90s decked out in grunge looks, so as much as I like the look on younger girls now, I don't feel like I can get away with it. ◆ I take inspiration from all around: music, movies, street-style photography, and other blogs. I'm always inspired by being in New York City, 60s French pop stars, and 30s pre-code Hollywood movies. ◆ I would never wear anything with words written across the butt or anything with obvious logos on it.

SÉBASTIEN TORUDU

BORN 1988 | FRENCH | CITY: PARIS | WWW.BOUCHEOUVERTE.BLOGSPOT.COM

SÉBASTIEN TORUDU

{ 11 THINGS ABOUT MYSELF }

Some of my friends call me Sebichou. ◆ I am a freelance photo and runway model. I have studied in a fashion design school because I want to become a fashion designer. ◆ I am quite shy and reserved. ◆ I am a big fan of Mickey Mouse. I think he's the love of my life. ◆ If he were human, only God knows what I would do with him, ha-ha. ◆ When I was a 6-year-old child, I watched a lot of American series from the 80s like Dallas, Dynasty or Knots landing. My love for fashion was born at this period of my life. I've decided to start creating women clothes. ◆ Since 2007, I've always dreamed of having a House Of Holland shirt and studded Repetto shoes designed by Comme des Garçons, but I never got either the shirt or shoes. I keep hope! ◆ I love laughing until I start choking or until I need to go pee. I love smiling. ◆ I think my blog is the mirror of my personality (it's poetical no?): a little crazy, a little shy, a little pop. ◆ My pants are always rolled up. ◆ I only need 2 minutes to choose an outfit.

TAHTI SYRJALA

BORN 1991 | FINNISH / AMERICAN | CITY : CORK | WWW.TAHTISYRJALA.BLOGSPOT.COM

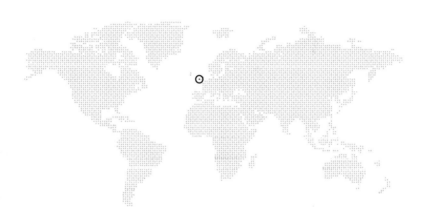

TAHTI SYRJALA

{ 12 THINGS ABOUT MYSELF }

I'm Finnish/American — my family moved to Ireland when I was five. Hence why I spell my name Tahti Syrjala, instead of the correct Tähti Syrjälä — it is just easier in an English-speaking country, which doesn't have the characters in their alphabet. However, Tahti also translates to the equivalent of "tempo" or "rhythm," so both translations work. ◆ I'm a natural redhead, and so is my sister — a case of very active recessive genes, as my mother is blonde and my father has black hair. ◆ I love food! Unlike the stereotype of fashionistas, I would prefer to go without a pair of shoes rather than miss a few meals! ◆ I began baking when I was nine — the very first thing I tried to bake were cinnamon buns. I tended to forget key ingredients such as eggs, though, in those early stages of learning! ◆ My blog has helped my self-esteem immensely. Until I began blogging I never had much confidence in my appearance — I had grown up in a very small, conservative town so I never received much positive feedback about my style. When I started posting my outfits and makeup, the compliments were quite overwhelming! ◆ My favorite movie is Requiem For a Dream. I saw it when I was fifteen, and I have watched it countless times since then. I think it is incredibly beautiful, eloquent, and moving. ◆ My favorite artists are Arthur Rackham and William Morris — I really respond to the muted color palette and the subtle intricacy of their work. ◆ My signature style would be structured, statement monochrome. I never wear neon. A muted color palette suits my skin tone and hair far better than brights. ◆ My favorite dish is my lemon tart. I adore very sour food, and it's seemingly impossible to eat without sweet cream. I eat it without, though! I dislike spicy food, but I love all the other three taste categories. ◆ I am right-handed, yet I am right-brained — my talents revolve around the categories of art and language. ◆ I sunburn incredibly easily, so in the summer months I stay indoors. Within five minutes of being exposed to the midday sun, I will have a nasty burn. ◆ I love makeup because it is the art of illusion. I used to paint myself with watercolors, since I was as young as three! This turned into a love for face painting, and then to makeup. I've been teaching myself since I was thirteen, and I recently decided to study it at college.

It was a perfect day today — gray and cool to moderate temperate, with no wind. I love to go for walks when it's like that, because there are rarely any people around to invade my solitude and silence.

LATAJACA PYZA

BORN 1979 | POLISH | CITY: MILAN | WWW.CHICANDCHEAP.BLOX.PL

LATAJACA PYZA

{ 6 THINGS ABOUT MYSELF }

I was born in Poland, but live now in Italy (Milan). ◆ I am an Internet addict. ◆ With my blog I want to have fun, be creative, and not take fashion too seriously. ◆ I keep changing my favorite colors and style as well as my mood. ◆ One of the things I learned thanks to being a fashion blogger is to say: Never say never. ◆ I would like to write a book or a movie screenplay one day.

ZOE DEMARUIS PORTIA FLOOD

BORN 1990 | AMERICAN | CITY: LOS ANGELES | WWW.GRANDTHEFTTHRIFT.BLOGSPOT.COM

ZOE DEMARUIS PORTIA FLOOD

{ 13 THINGS ABOUT MYSELF }

I am a model/fashion designer/stylist/cosmetologist/artist. ◆ I am of French, Vietnamese, and Mexican heritage. ◆ I live in downtown Los Angeles and love it! ◆ I can speak French fluently. ◆ I have been designing clothes since the age of 3 (doll clothes) and started designing real clothes when I was 11. ◆ I am a really big nerd. I love anime and video games. ◆ I had a really rough upbringing. I have been poor my whole life. ◆ I hardly ever spend more than 5 dollars on clothes, unless it's shoes, but still 25 dollars is my limit. ◆ I love cats. ◆ I am engaged to Steven Oviedo. ◆ I want to live in Paris some day. ◆ My blog is a place for me to share my creations and good thrifts I have gotten over the ages and to promote independent designers that are picking up the slack all on their own. I love to feature films or art that I love too. It is not a place where I post the same pictures of models and clothing that are unattainable to the public. ◆ I believe in being resourceful. If someone gives me a bag of undesirable clothing, I make it into something someone would want to actually buy. People need to look more at things to notice its potential instead of writing it off automatically.

Hey everyone!
I hope everyone
had a great
weekend!
I know I did!

ADRIAN FRANCIS WU

BORN 1990 | CHINESE | CITY: BURLINGTON/TORONTO | WWW.DAVISADRIAN.COM

ADRIAN FRANCIS WU

{ 16 THINGS ABOUT MYSELF }

I'm a dressmaker and somewhat of a designer ... I guess. ◆ I'm Chinese and 1/8 British ◆ I base my outfit around the bag I'm going to carry all day. ◆ I am a believer in love, and love is why we live. ◆ I taught myself how to sew and make dresses strictly from my head with no pattern-making. ◆ I wear "society-viewed women's clothing" because in the market men's clothes are crap. ◆ I'm a crazy extrovert that loves jazz, shopping, rock climbing, fashion, philosophy, opera, cheesy romantic movies, clubbing, and political discussions. ◆ I went to a private school, came out when I was 14 years old, and fell in love at age 18. ◆ I have a thing for wearing my chunky Ray-Ban glasses, and wearing wedges. ◆ I come off being very bubbly and happy when I'm not, at heart, frankly I'm quite cynical. ◆ I think its important to be a humble person. ◆ Androgyny is what inspires me. The idea of "neither man, neither woman." ◆ I push gender boundaries. From age 14 to the present, I have been on 50 dates with 50 different men — looking for love. ◆ I am a very complicated person. ◆ I love looking alien. ◆ I want to inspire people with my work. I want people to understand that there is more to fashion than being superficial. The waves and folds of my dresses are my dreams and thoughts colliding on command.

I'm Adrian. And I was brought up with a very fashionable mother and found myself quite fortunate to have so-called nice things. Every bag or designer piece I have is a possession of history.

NANCY ZHANG

BORN 1983 | CHINESE | CITY: BERLIN | WWW.XIAOXIZHANG.COM

NANCY ZHANG

{ 16 THINGS ABOUT MYSELF }

Nancy is my nickname. ◆ I currently live in Berlin. ◆ I do concept art and character design, illustration, comics, fashion pattern design. ◆ Once I think I want to finish one thing, I never give up. ◆ Actually I am quite sensitive, I worry about too many things. ◆ I love any beautiful things and like collecting them also. ◆ My idea and inspiration comes randomly; I like to draw them as illustration. ◆ My spirit lives in my dreamland ... sometimes. ◆ You will think I am quite a cold person from first glance in real life, but I am quite lively actually. ◆ I am a loyal Buddhist. That's why I always wear the beads in my fashion pics. ◆ I believe this world doesn't exist actually. Just like a dream. ◆ My character is close to a male's character. ◆ I love watching movies and listening to old-fashioned music. ◆ My blog always reminds me to work hard and create more of my drawings, ideas, and share more fashion pics with my readers. ◆ Positive feedback encourages me a lot. ◆ Anything on this planet could inspire me.

COCO

BORN 1981 | CANADIAN | CITY: VANCOUVER | WWW.OURPAPERMOON.BLOGSPOT.COM

COCO

{ 15 THINGS ABOUT MYSELF }

I am French Canadian: part-time Vancouverite, part-time Montrealer. ◆ I share a blog with my fiancé, Django. ◆ I am a hairdresser, a graphic designer, a finance wiz, a clothes lover, and a blogger. ◆ I am 4 feet 11 and 3/4 inches, but if you ask me I am 5 feet. ◆ Django and I share an impressive collection of books, including art and old illustration. It is where I take a lot of my inspirations. ◆ I am a shopper/blogger on a small budget. ◆ I am a reformed fashion eccentric. ◆ Django and I share the dream of owning a clothing, book, and home-ware boutique. ◆ I have had my hair every color imaginable, except for green. ◆ Everyone says that I'm the girliest girl they know, but I still see myself as a bit of a tomboy. ◆ It is very hard for me to let go of my old clothing; I'm thankful for generous attic space where I can go hunt to find some of my past treasures. ◆ I love so many different, distinct looks that I don't want to compromise one out of my wardrobe, thus creating my little mismatch style. ◆ Django and I love to explore new areas, shops, neighborhoods, and any type of vintage boutiques. ◆ Even if I sometimes love the look, I would never wear a cropped t-shirt. ◆ I have dreams of living on a boat, dressed in stripes and white pants every day.

SUNSHINE HURLBURT

BORN 1975 | AMERICAN | CITY: PHILADELPHIA | WWW.BLOGFULLOFJELLY.BLOGSPOT.COM

SUNSHINE HURLBURT

{ 12 THINGS ABOUT MYSELF }

Yes, Sunshine is my real name. ◆ I make ink drawings and ceramic sculptures. I crochet and sew and make all manner of crafty things. I collect and sell all things vintage. And I spend way too much time getting dressed! ◆ I work a few days a week at a vintage wholesale warehouse sorting through 1,000s of pounds of vintage clothing for the really good stuff. ◆ My latest endeavor is learning to make wheel-thrown pottery ... so soothing/frustrating/satisfying. ◆ I spent most of my childhood in south Florida, where everyone goes to retire and drop stuff at Goodwill. This is the land of amazing charity shops, which is why I started collecting vintage as soon as I was allowed to ride my bike out of the neighborhood. ◆ I obsessively watch old movies — dozens a week — ultimately hundreds of times each. ◆ There are 600+ movies made between 1928 and 1978 in this house. ◆ I'm a wicked cheapskate, unless it's something extremely frivolous like a giant Fendi backpack or white Chloe t-straps. I do love a good label, I won't lie. ◆ I live with a dog and two parakeets. ◆ I take my own pics. I have burned through quite a few cameras in the last 3 years! ◆ A friend once told me I always look like well-packaged Japanese candy. That stuck with me. ◆ I would never wear one of those velour tracksuits, anything that says anything across the bum, or flip-flops.

Pretty much always going for some sort of
secretary superhero look. Or candy witch.
Yeah that's it.

TAGHRID CHAABAN

LEBANESE | CITY: LOS ANGELES | WWW.TAGHRID.CC

TAGHRID CHAABAN

{ 13 THINGS ABOUT MYSELF }

I was born in Tripoli, Lebanon. ◆ My favorite color is Geranium Red. ◆ I don't really enjoy physically shopping. ◆ I love big bows on my head. ◆ I have a specific obsession with dance and jazz shoes. ◆ Belgian pudding is my favorite snack. ◆ Nour Chaaban, my sweet little sister, is my photographer. ◆ I love to draw and create things. ◆ I collect random magazines. ◆ I like feeling cute, proper, and feminine! ◆ The best purchase I have ever made is a vintage velvet jumpsuit. ◆ I'm a real girl, with a very real budget. With my blog I try to connect with other girls and women who are just like me. ◆ I try not to take myself too seriously.

JUAN COCCO

BORN 1989 | SPANISH | CITY: MADRID | WWW.MRJUANCOCCO.BLOGSPOT.COM

JUAN COCCO

I'm a simple curly-haired guy. ◆ I study law and economics in Madrid. ◆ I love skyscrapers, white chocolate, the cinema of the 90s, apple cakes, traveling, black comedy, and photography. ◆ When it comes to fashion I do not think I have any influence nor inspiration, or at least I try not to. I'd love to create my own style, a new and different one. Wouldn't it be great? ◆ I would never wear white jeans. ◆ I like all the clothes in my closet, so I usually choose the first tee I see. ◆ I wish we never die.

ELIZABETH

BORN 1986 | AMERICAN | CITY: ANCHORAGE, ALASKA | WWW.DELIGHTFULLY-TACKY.COM

ELIZABETH

Who am I? I am a vagabond from the great state of Alaska. I have a healthy affinity for 1970s Winnebagos, a creative spirit, and a love for the open road. My current occupation is graphic design. ◆ Soon I'm leaving Anchorage, Alaska, in my beloved 1973 Winnebago Brave to travel around the United States for an indefinite amount of time. Years ago I fell in love with 70s Braves and I think I've always loved the mobile lifestyle, so I'm making one of my life dreams come true by living on the road. I'll be blogging the whole time. ◆ I grew up in Anchorage, Alaska, which meant lots of winter fun, flying, watching the Iditarod, camping, wild animals chilling in our backyard, and so much more. ◆ I am a trekkie and have been to both a Star Trek convention in Las Vegas and on the set of the series Enterprise, where we got to meet the entire cast. It's kind of a family affair. My younger brother got into Star Trek in a big way and dragged us all in with him (we were willing accomplices, though). ◆ I rode horses competitively for about 11 years, competing in horse shows in Alaska and in California. My old room at home is full of ribbons and trophies. ◆ I majored in printmaking and someday I hope to set up a little press somewhere in my house (whenever I get a house and settle down, that is). ◆ I sometimes wish I could live life over again multiple times. I feel like there are too many things I want to do. ◆ I'm secretly wanting to become a forensic anthropologist. ◆ I'm quite a loner. I enjoy time to myself far more than time with other people, for the most part. I'm really quiet around other people, unless they are good friends, and then I can be quite the opposite. ◆ Avocados and wild Alaskan sockeye are my favorite foods. ◆ I love tacky, kitschy things, especially from the 1970s. My blog helped me to become a more confident and creative person. ◆ I'm always mixing prints. When I think about it, I guess I am! I never was taught any rules about fashion, so print mixing was never off limits to me and I kind of just do it automatically. ◆ The biggest style inspiration for me is other bloggers. I've never been able to relate to fashion magazines or celebrity style, so seeing real everyday girls looking chic and rocking cool trends is really inspiring.

Sometimes I just enjoy the simplicity of dresses. You can just put on a dress and be ready to go.

GEMMA ROWLANDS

BORN 1983 | BRITISH | CITY: NEW YORK | HTTP://FADETOBLACKNY.BLOGSPOT.COM

GEMMA ROWLANDS

{ 6 THINGS ABOUT MYSELF }

I'm a Leo, graphic artist, blogger, designer, shopping addict, and Brit. ◆ I was born in Gravesend (England). ◆ I moved to New York at 22. ◆ My blog is my own little space where I can express my creativity through my illustrations, designs, or daily outfits. It gives me a sense of freedom in a way ... I don't have to play by any rules. ◆ I love the beach. ◆ I hate the winter.

So Dudes, I will be 26 for only one more week. I turn a scary 27 on July 25th, but I would like to stay 26 if that's ok with you? So I'll be 26 for the next few years.

JIM DUMONT

BORN 1989 | FRENCH | CITY: LILLE | HTTP://ITSJIMTOT.WORDPRESS.COM

JIM DUMONT

{ 6 THINGS ABOUT MYSELF }

I'm a big vintage lover. ◆ I like to spend time in second-hand stores, garage sales, and flea markets looking for clothes, but also books and vinyl. ◆ I really enjoy creating pieces. I'm a DIY adept. ◆ In stores, there often are details on clothes that I don't like so I try to redo them my way, taking inspiration from what I've seen, but most of the time my imagination takes over and the final result is far away from my first idea. ◆ I collect a lot. I stopped counting how many sunglasses and hats I have ... ◆ Music is a big part of my life. I have pretty broad tastes but I listen mostly to rock/indie rock, but also new wave, psychedelic rock, etc.

COSETTE MUNCH

BORN 1991 | SWEDISH | CITY: MALMÖ | WWW.CRACK.BLOGG.SE

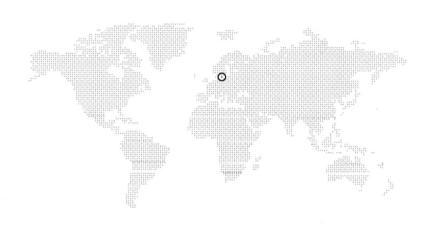

COSETTE MUNCH

{ 18 THINGS ABOUT MYSELF }

My full name is Cosette Munch Rebecca Ylva Karin Boqvist Bäckman. I attached Munch on my 18th birthday; Edvard Munch is my favorite artist and a big part of my life, so it suits me. Besides, I don't think anyone outside Sweden ever will be able to pronounce "Boqvist Bäckman," so I'm doing society a favor. ◆ I'm easy to find in vintage stores and in parks with a book and a cup of tea. ◆ When I'm frustrated, I throw fruit from bridges at night. I think I got that idea from Scrubs, but I'm not sure. ◆ I have tried all existing hair colors; my favorites are my current and blue. ◆ I must have some kind of headwear — hats, feathers, ribbons, anything. ◆ I can fold almost anything in the origami-world! Dinosaurs, cats, humans, flowers — you name it! ◆ Dinosaur t-shirts are the best kind of t-shirts! I think everyone should have one in their wardrobe. ◆ Everyone seems to think that I'm from Russia. I would love to know why. ◆ My biggest passions are music (Radiohead, Depeche Mode, Tom Waits), art (Edvard Munch, René Magritte, Gustav Klimt), and literature (George Orwell, Franz Kafka, Vladimir Nabokov). ◆ I have a thing for black and blue clothes. My favorite color match is red and blue, so blue clothes is a perfect match against my red hair. ◆ I am a sucker for tea and cakes. I could live the rest of my life with just that. ◆ If I see someone interesting on a bus, or hear something remarkable, I always write or sketch it down on my notepad. Probably my best companion. ◆ I always rub my feet against each other before I sleep. ◆ I just love to inspire people, in all matters. Just as I love to be inspired by others. ◆ I always wear winkle-pickers. I started to wear them when I was around ten and had a crush on Peter Murphy (he wears winkle-pickers in the "Telegram Sam" music video). I still have a crush on him, so I still wear winkle-pickers. ◆ I'm pretty shy, but when I see someone with clothing I love, I somehow get the power to ask where the person bought it. ◆ I think I have some kind of phobia against latex. ◆ I hardly ever wear small earrings. What's the use when they're invisible?

Every time I'm in Stockholm, I try to avoid rush hour as much as I can, mostly through one more cup of coffee at the sloppy café I probably visit, but want to get away from. I cannot cope with all people, not only because they are people, mostly because no one will remember another person's face.

NADIA

BORN 1984 | BRITISH | CITY: LONDON | WWW.FROUFROUU.COM

NADIA

{ 11 THINGS ABOUT MYSELF }

My hands and feet are always cold, to the point where I have to wear socks to bed. ◆
I wish Lacroix was still around. ◆ I daydream detailed, elaborately planned alternative
realities. ◆ I have an ever-expanding list of things I want to read and learn about, most of
which are as yet unread and unlearnt. ◆ I am a synesthete — I like to think this enhances
my view of the world. ◆ I am a fussy hoarder and a messy perfectionist. ◆ The concept of
hyperreality inspires me. ◆ My inspirations change frequently, along with my style, but my
longstanding influences are fictional and real characters from yesteryear (from Marchesa
Casati to Poirot), Czech New Wave, David Lynch's female leads, street style, women of the
60s (Pattie Boyd, Marianne Faithfull, Francoise Hardy), Baroque architecture, and Reme-
dios Varo. ◆ I enjoy people watching and observing their mannerisms. ◆ I subconsciously
draw with my fingers when my mind is preoccupied. ◆ I prefer wearing men's fragrances
to women's.

Any narratives
I volunteer would
probably not do
justice to the
thrilling time I had.

MIREIA

BORN 1979 | SPANISH | CITY: BARCELONA | WWW.MYDAILYSTYLE.ES

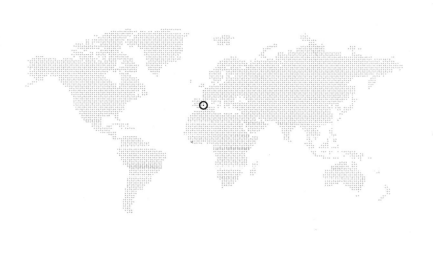

MIREIA

I'm a devoted mother of a little boy. ◆ I love reading; Cortázar is my favorite writer. ◆ I love watching series while eating popcorn. ◆ I love making collages from old fashion magazines. They really inspire me every time I look at them. ◆ I go shopping once per week, not only to shop, but to get inspiration. ◆ I have launched my own designs of swimsuits for children. ◆ I love photography. ◆ My favorite city is Paris, even though I think I could not live outside my hometown, Barcelona. Even when I lived in London for a year I missed it so much! ◆ I always try to be feminine. I do not understand trends that make women unattractive! ◆ My mother is my personal style icon. To me, she is the classiest woman alive.

KADEEM JOHNSON

BORN 1989 | AMERICAN | CITY: NEW YORK | WWW.KJOHNLASOUL.COM

KADEEM JOHNSON

{ 14 THINGS ABOUT MYSELF }

I'm a full-time college student and freelance photographer. I've been teaching myself the art of photography for the past 4 years now. ◆ I'm a pretty shy individual. ◆ I love walking around New York City and just getting lost. ◆ My favorite thing to do is thrift shop. I became addicted once I went away for school (great way of college budgeting). ◆ My favorite music is jazz and neo-soul. ◆ I'm just your average guy who also loves fashion. ◆ The style and essence of African-American people from the era of the Harlem Renaissance and the 1950s are my biggest fashion inspiration. ◆ My dream job is to work for a modeling agency. I've been into models and editorials for as long as I can remember. ◆ I love reading men's fashion magazines. ◆ My favorite thing to do is people-watch. I get most of my inspiration for pictures and style from the people around me. ◆ My blog means a great deal to me. Being that I don't speak much, it is my way of expressing myself through my images. Also, since I take so many pictures, having a blog is a great way of sharing what I see through my eyes. ◆ I would call my style afro-grunge. I don't really put too much though into what I wear. ◆ I MUST have a hat on my head. ◆ If I'm going out, I put together an outfit mentally while I'm in the shower. Therefore, when I get out I can just throw it on and leave the house with no stress.

I don't talk much,
so I will speak
through the images
that I post.

KEIKO LYNN GROVES

BORN 1984 | AMERICAN/JAPANESE | CITY: NEW YORK | WWW.KEIKOLYNN.COM

KEIKO LYNN GROVES

{ 14 THINGS ABOUT MYSELF }

My name is pronounced "cake-oh." Some people call me Baby Keiks, Panda, Keiks, Unicorn, and a plethora of others. Almost no one calls me Keiko, but when being called by my actual name I prefer Keiko Lynn. ◆ I am honest, awkward, and downright whimsical. ◆ I'm not a teeny tiny girl but I know how to dress for my body shape. ◆ I'm pigeon-toed. It was extreme when I was little but I wore corrective braces and shoes. I'm still a little pigeon-toed and get called out on it all the time. ◆ I always, always, always spill something when I'm eating or drinking. I'm extremely clumsy. ◆ My signature style is vintage with a twist of whimsy. People tell me all the time that I look like "a little dress up doll." ◆ I'm 1/4 Japanese, which is how I got the name Keiko. ◆ At 5' 7", I tower over my dad's side of the family, some men included. To everyone else, I'm average height. ◆ Animals are a huge part of my life. I grew up with a zoo of animals and feel more comfortable with a horse than any person. My social life has been a struggle because of this; my friend recently told me, "You've carried Animal Kingdom citizenship for over a decade." It's actually been 25 years and I don't know if that's ever going to change. ◆ I only know two languages: English and American Sign Language. Deaf culture absolutely fascinates me. ◆ I have never spent over $50 on a single garment or accessory, ever. ◆ I have four sisters, no brothers, and grew up with a single (and very young) mom. ◆ I originally majored in musical theater before transitioning to fashion. I have no formal training in fashion. ◆ I used to hate dresses and everything girly; I didn't start wearing them until college. Now, I almost always wear dresses or skirts. My teenage self would be appalled.

From time to time, I've thought about doing a "what's in my bag" post, but then I remember that I can't fit that much stuff in one frame.

ANJA LOUISE VERDUGO

BORN 1983 | CANADIAN | CITY: PORTLAND, OREGON | WWW.CLEVERNETTLE.COM/BLOG

ANJA LOUISE VERDUGO

{ 13 THINGS ABOUT MYSELF }

I am obsessed with hunting morel mushrooms in the spring. I think they put some kind of spores into my brain that causes me to desire them in an almost crazy way. They are the most delicious mushrooms in the world. ◆ I grew up in British Columbia and have a soft spot for the Northwest and old photos of people camping in that area. Little old plaid nerds! ◆ My fabric scrap collection is threatening to take over the basement. I hem a lot of skirts and dresses with great prints for my vintage shop, and I can't bear to toss out the fabric. So, the mountain grows ... ◆ I'm a vintage collector/lover/dealer/nerd. ◆ I frequently have dreams where I am searching through abandoned houses or old towns that are filled with amazing treasures. I'm always disappointed when I wake up and all the great old stuff disappears. ◆ I drink a lot of tea. ◆ I am endlessly interested in secret societies, fraternal orders, and brotherhoods. I love stealing their imagery for my art and collecting antique society paraphernalia. ◆ My best purchase is a handmade 1960s winter coat with a tapestry print and furry trim. I call it my "couch coat." ◆ My little family consists of my husband Dalas, our cat 56, parrotlet Cigarette, and two chickens — Scramble and Bunny. ◆ My favorite fashion eras are the 20s/30s and the 1960s. I love when worlds collide, especially if a 1920s dress looks a little psychedelic. ◆ The squirrel is my favorite animal. ◆ I mainly shop at thrift stores. ◆ Above all, I love jokes and laughing with people who are on the same wavelength. What could be better?

SHAN SHAN

BORN 1979 | CHINESE | CITY: OSAKA | HTTP://WEBBLOG.TINYTOADSTOOL.COM

SHAN SHAN

{ 15 THINGS ABOUT MYSELF }

I am a housewife and textile artist, and I have two online shops (one for crafts and one for clothes). Sometimes I write articles in the fashion and textile magazine. ◆ I am 164 cm. ◆ My favorite movie is Billy Elliot. ◆ My favorite brand is Comme des Garçons. ◆ I want to keep a cat. ◆ Red is my soul color. ◆ I am correcting my teeth. ◆ I can't live without making something. ◆ I would never wear slim pants — they don't suit my legs! ◆ I grew up at the seaside but can't swim. ◆ I wasn't a bright girl in childhood but I liked to show myself brightly. ◆ I care about how others look at me, but I like to go my way. ◆ I want to open my own vintage shop and café in the future. ◆ My various stockings are the key pieces of my wardrobe. ◆ My best purchase ever made is a white vintage dress.

KARL PHILIP LEUTERIO

BORN 1987 | FILIPINO | CITY: MANILA | WWW.TOTALLYINKARLCERATING.BLOGSPOT.COM

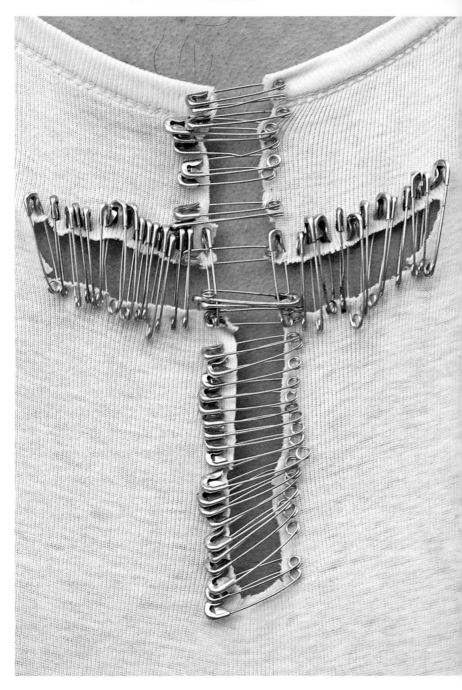

KARL PHILIP LEUTERIO

{ 8 THINGS ABOUT MYSELF }

I am a registered nurse. ◆ Fashion keeps me sane. ◆ My blog is my haven, my treasure chest, my moodboard, and my online diary where 5 billion people or above are welcome to read it. ◆ I wear a lot of black. ◆ I am inspired by skinny Swedish, British, and Parisian guys who wear weird outfits and still make it work. ◆ If I am gonna go out, I prepare three hours before. ◆ I think fashion and music are inseparable. ◆ My only fashion rule is to never take it too seriously or you'll end up with overkill.

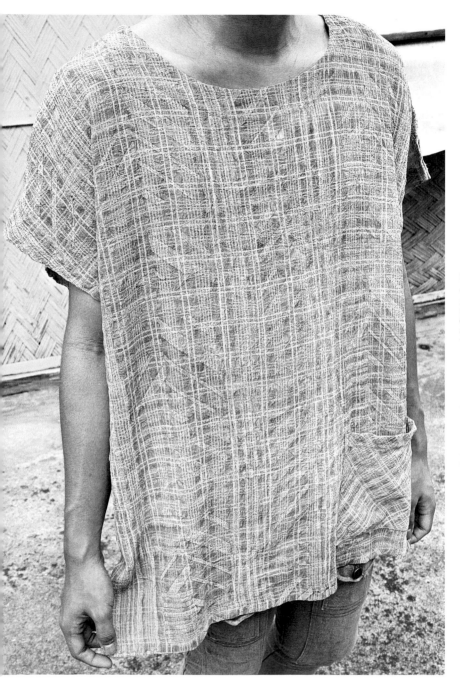

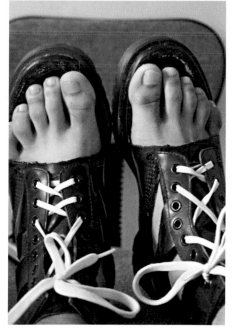

FLORA WISTRÖM

BORN 1994 | SWEDISH | CITY: STOCKHOLM | HTTP://FLORASBLOGG.SE

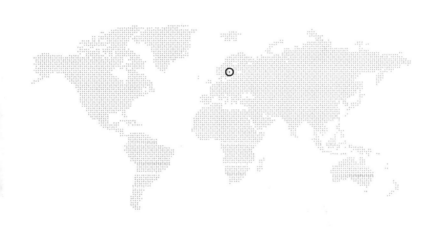

FLORA WISTRÖM

{ 10 THINGS ABOUT MYSELF }

I love to travel. I like to draw, I like to write, I like to photograph. ✦ I don't like people who think that they are better than others. ✦ I love talking about love. ✦ I am a romantic person. ✦ For me, it is important to be personal, genuine, and proper while blogging. ✦ I started school one year earlier. ✦ I am quite a wild person. ✦ I almost always walk around with a smile. ✦ My blog is a diary for me. I love looking back in the archive (even though I look terrible in older photos) and remember how my life used to be before. ✦ I always choose clothes the night before. Otherwise my whole morning would be choosing clothes.

CARRIE HARWOOD

BORN 1990 | BRITISH | CITY: SOMERSET/LONDON | WWW.WISHWISHWISH.NET

CARRIE HARWOOD

My real home is in Somerset — not well renowned for it's Fashion, however it's also the birthplace of Mulberry! ◆ Before I started studying fashion promotion, I had always planned on becoming a graphic designer. ◆ I use a Canon 400D to take all of my photographs — a frequently asked question! ◆ I have an unhealthy obsession with collecting old junk; my desk is covered with teddy bears that nobody else wanted and miniature tea sets. ◆ If I'm in a hurry before university, I'll wear something safe, like a dress with tights and flats, but if it's the weekend I'll be a little more adventurous and try out new combinations. I usually pick one item that I want to include and then build the rest of the outfit around it, based on fabric and color. Although I'm never that strict, creating an outfit should be fun, not about following rules! ◆ It takes a whole wardrobe and 4 vintage suitcases to hold all of my clothing. ◆ The first blog I ever started reading was Galadarling.com. ◆ I'm also crazy for pretty packaging and letters — I love writing to pen pals. ◆ I love 60s French Nouvelle Vague films, so of course Anna Karina is a huge style icon for me. ◆ Everything I want to share with the world is posted on my blog. ◆ The most expensive item in my wardrobe is my Mulberry Alexa, costing a crazy £795. ◆ Before I started blogging, I used to dance in my spare time. Ballet was my favorite! ◆ The best thing about the blogosphere is the feeling that a positive comment can give you, or the thought of being in a huge community of like-minded people — it's amazing how many great people I've met thanks to blogging. Of course, on the flipside, a single negative comment from an anonymous reader can put you in a bad mood for the rest of the day. When your blog is something you put your heart into, it's upsetting when people can so easily come along and tell you they hate what you're doing. ◆ I couldn't live without a striped Breton top and a classic trench coat! Similarly, I won't be seen without my Alexa bag, it's glued to my hand! Other wardrobe staples include peg-leg trousers and vintage dresses with peter-pan collars. ◆ I once interviewed TV Stylist Gok Wan.

A trip anywhere wouldn't be complete without a bit of posing at a picturesque location — or maybe that's just us bloggers!

ADAM GALLAGHER

BORN 1991 | AMERICAN | CITY: RIVERSIDE, CALIFORNIA | HTTP://WHATDREAMZ.BLOGSPOT.COM

ADAM GALLAGHER

{ 16 THINGS ABOUT MYSELF }

I have high aspirations to be in the fashion industry. Currently I am interning as a stylist and getting my foot in the door. I love the experience, it's surreal and inspiring! Being around models everyday and photographers is exactly what I want to wake up to as my profession. ◆ I also model (hoping to be represented by an agency soon!). ◆ I'm a huge animal lover. ◆ Volleyball is my favorite sport. ◆ I sang in high school, and was asked to attend the national honor choir of the USA. ◆ I am surprised at how many people came to love what I had to say in my blog or captured through photographs, because I was always picked on growing up for my weird sense of style and personality. ◆ Mac 'n' cheese has got to be the best food. ◆ I know sign language. ◆ I used to think I took forever getting ready, but I was proved wrong once I got into the fashion scene where they take hours at a time just on makeup and hair. ◆ I'm moving to LA. ◆ My fashion icons from the past include Andy Warhol, Michael Jackson, Bob Fosse. And the 20s era is just stunning in my opinion. ◆ My mom is my best friend. ◆ I'm a huge romantic. ◆ I drive a Honda Accord. ◆ I don't necessarily have a "signature style," but I do favor a lot of blacks and band tee shirts. ◆ My style is inspired by everything around me, whether it's somebody, something, or somewhere. I try to never conform to society's trends and march to the beat of my own drummer.

Hello my fashionistas! How are you guys doing?

CAROLINA ENGMAN

SWEDISH | CITY: STOCKHOLM | WWW.FASHIONSQUAD.COM

CAROLINA ENGMAN

{ 7 THINGS ABOUT MYSELF }

I work as a stylist and study fashion at the University of Stockholm. ◆ A perfect day would be a picnic at the park together with friends in the sun. ◆ I've been collecting tons of inspirational pictures since I was a kid and have always loved to write, so I thought why not share this with others? That's when I started my blog. ◆ My style is simple yet chic, with a little bit of rock going on. ◆ My room is literally a big fashion mess. There are clothes, shoes, and bags all over the place, so when I get dressed in the morning I just dig up something that looks good. ◆ My favorite color is dark blue. ◆ I am shy.

FRIDAY. May all
your dreams come
true! xx

© Prestel Verlag, Munich · Berlin · London · New York 2010

© of all photos by the individual bloggers, 2010, with the exception of the following:
Scott McBee: pp. 70, 79 bottom left; Lars Stephan (www.larsstephan.com): pp. 72, 76, 77, 78, 79 top;
Justin Williams (www.thedocumentarist.com): pp. 74, 75; Nicholas Turner: p. 79 bottom right;
Filip Tot: pp. 138, 140, 142, 143, 144, 145, 146, 147, 148, 149, 150, 151; Jennifer Martin: pp. 188 bottom, 193;
Tom Bejgrowicz (www.tombphotography.tumblr.com): pp. 184, 186, 188 top, 189, 190, 191, 192;

Cover: Audrey Leighton Rogers, see page 132
Frontispiz: Karl Philip Leuterio, see page 360
Back Cover: Adrian Frances Wu, see page 226

Prestel, A member of Verlagsgruppe Random House GmbH

Prestel Verlag
Königinstraße 9
80539 Munich
Tel. +49 (89) 24 29 08 300
Fax +49 (89) 24 29 08 335
www.prestel.de

Prestel Publishing Ltd.
4, Bloomsbury Place,
London WC1A 2QA
Tel. +44 (20) 7323-5004
Fax +44 (20) 7636-8004
www.prestel.com

Prestel Publishing
900 Broadway, Suite 603
New York, N.Y. 10003
Tel. +1 (212) 995-2720
Fax +1 (212) 995-2733
www.prestel.com

Library of Congress Control Number: 2010933778

British Library Cataloguing-in-Publication Data
A catalogue record for this book is available from the British Library.

The Deutsche Bibliothek holds a record for this publication in the Deutsche Nationalbibliografie;
detailed biographical data can be found under: http://dnb.ddb.de

Prestel books are available worldwide. Please contact your nearest bookseller
or one of the above addresses for information concerning your local distributor.

Editorial direction by **Claudia Stäuble**
Assistance by **Regina Herr**
Copy-edited by **Jonathan Fox**, Barcelona
Cover and layout concept by **Benjamin Wolbergs**, Berlin
Production by **Astrid Wedemeyer**
Art direction by **Cilly Klotz**
Origination by **ReproLine Mediateam,** München
Printing and binding by Tlaciarne BB, spol. sr.o.

Verlagsgruppe Random House FSC-DEU-0100
The FSC-certified paper *Eurobulk* produced by
mill Biberist has been supplied by Papier Union.

ISBN: 978-3-7913-4474-4 (English edition)
978-3-7913-4475-1 (German edition)

FSC
Mixed Sources
Product group from well-managed
forests and other controlled sources
Cert no. SGS-COC-004236
www.fsc.org
© 1996 Forest Stewardship Council